Hampton Loade

Figure 1 The Hampton Loade Ferry, commissioned by
David Browning and hand drawn by Angie Dunn.

Hampton Loade

the land that time (nearly) forgot

Kate Creed

BREWIN BOOKS

First published by
Brewin Books Ltd, 56 Alcester Road,
Studley, Warwickshire B80 7LG in 2011

www.brewinbooks.com

© Kate Creed 2011

ISBN: 978-1-85858-474-4

A Cataloguing in Publication Record
for this title is available from the British Library.

Typeset in Verdigris
Printed in Great Britain by
Cambrian Printers.

Table of Contents

List of Figures

Introduction

Today we are so fortunate to have followed generations of people who have recorded their present, we may have to dig deep to find these records but they do exist and are waiting to be found and put together for us: the like minded who enjoy the journey of not only looking at where we are going but enjoy a glimpse back to what has gone before. This journey gives the reader a peek into the past and a gentle probe into life trials, tribulations, changes and difficulties which led to the ultimate survival of this beautiful Shropshire spot.

There is no other single work that explores the hamlet in isolation and this work travels across the river, down the river, alongside it and occasionally under it. It tells tales of industrial commerce and private enterprise, the life and times of the iron works and the old public houses. It is mindful of those who had the foresight to make some necessary changes in the village and those who have had the good grace to accept changes imposed upon them. There is undoubtedly more to uncover, there always is in a work such as this. History never stops being created and its perspective is subjective to which side of the river we happen to be standing on. It is therefore important to just pause for a moment in time and record some of it and not attempt more, it records a view and is not attempting in any way to be the definitive article. It covers a diverse range of subject matter; including the old Iron works and its place beside the prominent names of the industrial revolution, the ferry, the bridge, the railway and three public houses, The River and Rail, The Unicorn and The Lion.

I hope this proves to be as interesting to the reader as it has been to me in compiling it.

Kate Creed

Acknowledgments

This work began life in 2007 as a leaflet for those interested in the historic hamlet of Hampton Loade. It was then apparent that it was developing into a booklet as there were so many offers of information and pictures coming to light which historically should not be ignored, it became difficult to know how to filter or exclude the information as it is all so interesting and pertinent to the what was fast becoming a major project. "It is" therefore now "what it is", a study, a leaflet, a book, a historic walk and nostalgic journey and lastly, for me a delight to have created. The people of Hampton Loade have contributed and been a constant reminder to me of what needs to be done and have been consistently encouraging making the right kind of gentle criticisms.

Thanks are also due to the staff of numerous libraries and record offices, in particular at the Shropshire Records and Research Centre, Bridgnorth library and; The Alveley Historical society.

The English Heritage Trust.
Bing and Joyce Cooper.
David Browning.
Harriet Creed.
Karen and Clive Austin.
Keith and Sue Brettle.
Roger Brown.
Omar Aguao.
Hilary Fewtrell.
Tom White.
Mr D. H Dillon.
Sid and Joyce Link.
Bridgnorth Library.
The Severn Valley Railway.
Hazel Mottershed.
Taylor & Francis Books (UK).

To name but a few, I intend to omit no contributors here but if there are any omissions please accept my profuse apologies and sincere thanks to each and every one person who made this possible.

Foreword

Hampton Loade, the land that time (nearly) forgot

I have taken a longstanding interest in preserving the ferry services at Hampton Loade. I was therefore pleased to be invited to contribute a foreword to this fascinating history of the wider hamlet of Hampton Loade itself.

Chronicling the history of the hamlet and the lives of some of those caught up in that history, whether as workers, ferrymen or landowners is important, providing as it does a lasting record of the origins and development of this remarkable living piece of Shropshire's history.

Kate Creed takes us on a journey, an interesting and unique investigation, reflecting through time the importance in people's lives on the river, the three public houses, the ferry, and the bridge, the latter provoking an intriguing insight into its origin and reflecting the development of the hamlet through an industrial revolution.

The recorded heritage of this hamlet is a reminder to us all of the endeavour, ingenuity and fortitude of our predecessors, many of whose roles changed over time from tilling the soil to toiling in the emerging industrial landscape, during an era when day to day life was hard but simple, yet not softened by the comforts of our modern world.

Hampton Loade, the land that time (nearly) forgot is an interesting glimpse into the past and local history. Residents and visitors alike will thank Kate Creed for recording this history of this beautiful stretch of the Severn River valley.

By Philip Dunn MP for Ludlow

D'Hampton – A History

The tales, the records and the archives, just waiting to be found.

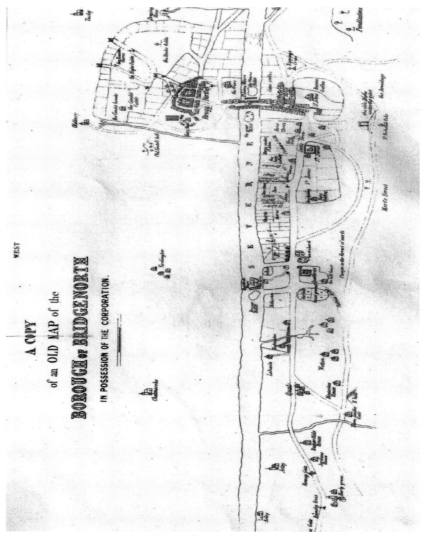

Figure 2 **Old Bridgnorth Map, undated.**
**This old undated map clearly shows Chelmarsh and Alveley but bears
no mention of Hampton Loade.**

The residents of today live in the Hamlet for quite different reasons from their forbearers, the farmers and iron-workers who once resided there: but I would imagine they would all share the common view that this is a precious spot. Many of the existing residents have lived in Hampton Loade for many years, they have tales to tell and have memories to share. These oral histories are valuable, precious and worthy however trite they appeared in the making, they now serve as a picture where there is no other record into this ever changing riverside hamlet.

The archives in Bridgnorth provided documents about the old Iron works that once stood there in a busy community that left behind only a silent wall and the

Figure 3 **A view of the Hamlet along the lane.**

echoes of men who toiled by day and night to keep a family fed, what has become of that history? Well, this is no definitive tome but it provides us with some tales of the land and its people. It also visits a time of exciting engineering trials and testing, stories of difficult times both on the river and off without forgetting the lands and its inhabitants on either side of the river. The libraries at Kidderminster and the archives in Shropshire hold newspaper records, books, land records of lands and their owners, people, farms and workers all of which were just waiting to be released to you the reader, whose interest goes beyond the role that newspapers so often play, those interested in our past and heritage. The Alveley history society has provided photographs after many years of collecting and allowed access to local records from families' histories, through their valuable publications. The Bridgnorth Journal has also been a rich source of information about local history; it takes a while to trawl through them all which go back to the mid 1800s, but it has been well worth it. All these resources help provide a rich and varied history that exceeds the boundaries of the hamlet to touch; the industrial revolution, English film makers, breweries, courts, railways enthusiasts, fishermen, walkers and picnickers alike. It's a journey that goes beyond the river and the railway exploring lives, loves, losses and laws, enjoy it's going to be memorable trip.

Geographically the picturesque Hamlet of Hampton Loade is securely nestled along the River Severn hiding between Kidderminster and Bridgnorth. The ecclesiastical boundaries of the hamlet are divided between the parishes of Chelmarsh and Alveley. The hamlet is in the post code district of Wolverhampton and in the local government district of Bridgnorth, which is four miles to the north. It is in the parliamentary constituency of Ludlow and the West Midlands European parliament constituency. On a less formal note it's also in many guide and tourist books as the quintessentially English beauty spot and receives much attention for its ferry, frequent floods and the railway station, however, there is a lot more to Hampton Loade historically than is ever given credit for. Hampton Loade station is actually located on the Hampton side of the river on the western bank and Hampton Loade is on the eastern bank. It is also recorded as Hampton, Hempton and Hemptons Loade, I suspect it depended on your perspective, your spelling and your allegiance. Confusing yes of course it is, just like the all districts, areas and postal address, why make it easy?

The ancient family names of Hampton Loade

The De Hampton family

At the commencement of the 14th century brothers Simon and William De Hampton had each purchased parts of Alveley. William later purchased further land from Ralph Noel around 1255 and by 1284 De Hamptons owned one sixth of a knight's fee in Alveley.

More ancient family names of Hempton 1557

Doode of Hempton
Wilkes family of Hempton .
Cook of Hempton. James of Hempton. Doyve of Hempton. Spencers of Hempton, Crofte of Hempton.
Foxall of Hempton. Longjon of Hempton and not forgetting the Whitmore's of Hampton Loade.

The family of Wolryche, Whitmore

Dudmaston Hall, home to the Wolryche-Whitmore family who for many generations leased the land that provided the iron works to Hampton Loade.

The land is suggested to be home to a Knight from the twelfth century when "Dudmaston was granted a half a hide of land by King Henry I to Hubert Fitz Helcot of Castle Holgate in Corvedale and by him to a Harlewyn de Butailles, who then took the name to the place De Dudmaston". The deed survives and was produced prior to 1127. His descendant, the De Dudmaston heiress Margaret, married William Wolryche in 1403 (National Trust). It was Sir Thomas Wolryche that built the present house although there is a lack of information about this era as very few documents survived this era.

Further down the family tree Mary Wolryche left Dudmaston to her uncle, her mother's brother, Colonel Thomas Weld. After his death in 1774 it passed to George Whitmore who died the following year without heirs. It then passed to William Whitmore of Southampton. The connection between the Wolryche and Whitmore families came about through Ann Weld the sister of George Weld who was Mary Wolryche's grandfather and Colonel Thomas Weld's father who had married Richard Whitmore of Lower Slaughter, George Whitmore's grandfather (National Trust).

Descendant William Whitmore, a Whig MP and fierce advocate of the repeal of the Corn Laws, passed the house to his sister's son and subsequently her grandson Geoffrey Wolryche-Whitmore. In 1952 he made most of the estate over to Lady Rachel Labouchere, who gave it to the National Trust in 1978.

Dudmaston Hall and Lands

Dudmaston Hall is one of the National Trust Properties and was acquired in 1978. The hall was given by the great Lady Labouchere who was the fifth great granddaughter of the famous Abraham Darby. Abraham Darby was the famous Quaker ironmaster of Coalbrookdale during the world's great Industrial Revolution which resulted in the building of the first Iron Bridge. You will find items from the Darby's at Dudmaston and at Rosehill House and Dale House (in Ironbridge). Not only was Lady Labouchere a descendent of the Darby's, she was also a descendent of the Wolryche Whitmore family. The Darby Room shows the family tree connecting the important families of the time; Darby's of Coalbrookdale, Christy's, Fells, and Wolryche-Whitmore's of Dudmaston.

Dudmaston has been in continuous family ownership since 1126. Sir George and Lady Labouchere lived at the hall for 40 years and have left a lasting influence on how the hall looks today.

Because Lady Labouchere was the fifth generation granddaughter of Abraham Darby and was herself a Quaker, Lady Labouchere was president of the Ironbridge Gorge Trust from 1973-1987 and instrumental in saving the Darby houses from dereliction. Lady Labouchere died March 22, 1996, aged 87 at Dudmaston.

An extract:

Mr. Whitmore's motion respecting the Corn Laws

26 *February* 1823
Mr. Whitmore moved for leave to bring in a bill for lowering the price, at which the importation of foreign corn was permitted, by 2s. a year, until it was reduced to 60s. Mr. Huskisson (the new President of the Board of Trade) opposed the motion.

Mr. Ricardo said, that the right hon. gentleman, in all the arguments which he had brought forward for postponing the consideration of the corn laws, had in reality given a reason for proceeding at once to amend them. What was the danger which his hon. friend, who brought forward the present motion, apprehended? It was the danger of those very high prices, to the recurrence of which the right hon. gentleman looked forward, as the conjuncture when the Corn Laws might be amended. He apprehended the danger of capital being again drawn, by the temptation of high prices, to the land (and the right hon. gentleman agreed that the danger existed)— that there would again be a succession of low prices, and another loss of capital. This evil it was the object of the present proposition to prevent; yet the right hon. gentleman would wait till the evil came upon them, before he would provide the remedy. As to the motion of his hon. friend, he would not oppose it; because he should be glad of any approach to a free trade in corn. But he thought his hon. friend did not go far enough; he had left the mischief of a fixed price. Both his hon. friend and the right hon. gentleman had laid down the true principles of a corn law; namely, that a protecting duty should be imposed on foreign corn, equal to the peculiar burthens borne by the grower of corn in this country. But, when this was done, a fixed price should be done away altogether. In fact his hon. friend had seemed a little uncertain as to his fixed price. He had taken it at 60s; but he had stated that if foreign corn could be imported at 55s, he should have reduced it to that. He thought he had committed a great error in taking any fixed price at all. A duty should be imposed on corn imported, equal to the peculiar burthens borne by the grower of corn; and, in his opinion, a drawback or bounty to nearly the same amount should be allowed on corn exported. Then, and then only, would corn be kept at a price nearly equal in this, to what it was in other countries. If there was an abundant harvest, it would find a vent by means of the bounty; and, on the other hand, if there was a deficient supply, under the influence of the duty, corn would be introduced as it was wanted, and not in the enormous quantities poured in under the existing law, when the price rose to a certain height. [...].

The object of the approach to a free trade, which he recommended, was to keep prices steady and low. He did not mean such low prices as would not remunerate the grower; for when the manufacturer ate his bread at all cheaper than the price at which the farmer could be remunerated, the greatest injury was done to the general interests of the country.

The House divided on the motion: Ayes, 25; Noes, 78. Ricardo voted for the motion.

Church Records

The Church records of Chelmarsh reveal a number of tragic events in the parish, which, when read beside the problems we have today, have a humbling effect upon the reader. These people died of suffering: disease, malnutrition, neglect and infections. One set of parents lost two new born babies within one year; another wife lost her mother, her husband and her baby within a month of each other. One father buried two sons in the same week and within a year he too was in the record book as a burial. On Jan 23rd 1797 a 'travelling 'poor man' by the name of Richard Burgess died in the hamlet, no cause of death is revealed in the registers but when he is labelled a 'poor man' we can only imagine his circumstances. Many a married couple parted by death seem to be reunited in death very quickly demonstrating how much life itself can often depend on the existence of another, particularly in close knit families and communities.

Our current society's problems with obesity and antibiotic resistant infections seem a full pendulum swing away, the results are the same, the losses are as tragic to the family and friends, but the reasons for the losses are quite different. It would be an interesting to see how they would view our debts, obsession with consumerism and health problems of today.

A Raft for all Reasons
The Hampton Loade Ferry

The unique passenger foot ferry is a rare reaction cable ferry which links the two sides of Hampton Loade, separated by the River Severn.

Figure 4 **The 16th Century Ferry Crossing point. An undated Picture courtesy of Alveley historical society.**

The river crossing at Hampton Loade has been in use for around 400 years, and may even have provided a route across the Severn during Medieval times. A reference to 'Hemptons Loade' can be traced back to 1594, and name 'Loade' is in fact an Old English word meaning ford or river crossing. Geology and terrain were major factors for both the iron forges and the ancient ferry crossing at the hamlet and each provided for the other. It is one of the last surviving ferries on the river Severn. William Whitmore leased the ferry and the forge to John Thompson then of Lye Hall, Alveley in 1797 for 21 years at £45.00 per year, along with a licence to erect forges and engines on the land. The closure of the iron works left the Whitmore Company still operating the ferry when its clerks and agents were exempt from toll. The rights to operate the ferry were purchased again from the late Captain Wolryche Whitmore of Dudmaston Hall near Bridgnorth by the James's.

This extract from Rob Whittle's memories of the village explains how the ferry works:

"The ferry is operated by water power; a strong overhead cable carries a pulley which is attached to the ferry. The tiller on the ferry turns into the fast flowing river and as the current pushes the ferry it crosses from one side to the other. The sighting of the ferry and the ford was down to the geology of the river bed, the river on upstream side of the ferry runs 6 - 10 feet deep for about a mile north. As it comes to the ferry and the ford the river bed rises as it hits the solid rock bottom, with a river depth at summer levels of three feet and lower. The river not only speeds up as it hits the shallow rock bed, but gains massive power. This power is then used to push the ferry from one side of the river to the other. The road into Hampton Loade used to go all the way down to the river edge but these days the concrete bollards forbid such a journey, the bollards in place because motorists mistook the glimmer of the river on dark wets nights as a wet greasy road and just carried on driving: the residents have many a tale to tell about helping to retrieve cars and passengers from rather damp and unwelcome adventures. The old ford which once carved its way across the river, taking the carts, horses and more latterly the odd car has long gone but what does remain in Hampton Loade is the historic ferry.

Figure 5 **Horses at Hampton Loade.**
This is a photograph of a team of horses hauling timber across the ford at Hampton Loade; it is understood to have been taken by Mr A. D. Chambers of Kidderminster in 1892.

Recorded as being in operation for hundreds of years this historic ferry would have many a tale to tell if it could talk. Newspapers have recorded more recent history for us and whilst it's not all good news it helps place its importance of the role it has played and continues to play in the community" (Whittle).

Rob Whittle continues: "From as long ago as man needed to cross the river right through to the days of the industrial revolution the River Severn has been used as a byway in the way we use a motorway today. The fords that crossed the river became a barrier in dry summer conditions; they would stop the heavy barges, which would get stuck on the shallow bed of the fords. It was not long before the ferryman also became the ford keeper. A temporary type of lock was required to raise the level of the river over the ford bed every time a heavy barge needed to navigate the ford at low summer levels. This temporary lock was accomplished by sighting a row of two foot square by six foot high posts; they were fixed into the riverbed on the downstream side of the ford, just as the riverbed began to deepen. Holes were chiselled out of the solid rock bed, the holes were several feet deep to hold a two foot square oak post that was six foot high above the river bed. The posts were sighted six feet apart from one side of the river to about thirty feet from the opposite bank. The ford keeper would then with help from the bargees put up heavy oak planks up against the oak posts on the upstream side. This would raise the river level over the ford to allow the barges to get through the thirty foot gap, near the far bank. After the barges had passed by, the ford needed to be reopened, so a team of horses using ropes would be used to remove the heavy oak from the posts. The horses were used because of the huge water pressure on the boards, caused as the river level was raised.

The ford keeper would receive a fee for each barge that used the temporary system, so with his revenue from both the ferry and the ford he could make a fair living. Most of the barges and Severn trowes carrying iron travelled between Ironbridge and Stourport on the River Severn, they would join the canal system to take their cargos to the Black Country for machining. If you walk the river Severn between Stourport and Ironbridge on the western bank, you will see that every river, stream or brook and trickle of water, has a bridge or a culvert over it as it enters the River Severn. The reason for this was that the big barges and Trowes needed to be pulled back up stream against the river current. Every tree close to the Severn was cut down and all the tributaries bridged, this then allowed teams of horses to pull the barges back upstream to Ironbridge. Farmers along the Severn did big business, supplying fresh teams of horses for the barges.

The first cottage of the Severn Terrace in the hamlet is recorded as being the ferryman's cottage. The cottage was rebuilt in the 1980s; the original was built in sandstone c1570 which is indicative in itself of how long the ferry has been in operation. It was one of the three buildings in the hamlet, the others being the Lion Public house and Lye Hall, (figure 14) the remainder of the buildings grew around the Iron Forge. The ferry man's cottage was home to Bill and Clara Parkes in the 1950s and early 1960s. Clara ran a little cafe and sweet shop for the fisherman and the tourists. The other cottages at that time were homes to the Jellyman family and to Les Link, who did many of the odd jobs around the hamlet; he could do anything from painting to building. The family name of Link is strong in this tiny hamlet as there was a Sid and Joyce Link and an Edith Link all occupying separate dwellings. It was Edith who was in possession of two oil paintings of Hampton Loade during the 1800s, which remain in the hamlet. Edith was said to be the "Queen of Hampton Loade" she was 93 when she left the village to go to a nursing home in Bridgnorth and died there at the age of 97. Her son Cyril lived not too far away in Quatt, but she still at times became a little lonely. When I returned home from school she used to call me in for a chat, I would climb down the wooden stairs to her back door and she used to tell me first hand of all her childhood memories of Hampton Loade. It was Cyril who found the two oil paintings of Hampton Loade in the Victorian age and on the back were two messages, "please give these to Mr Whittle of The Lion Inn". I still have them and the messages are still pinned to the back! The next cottage along is now called Post Cottage and was occupied by Mr and Mrs Bert Pitt, Bert was a gardener for the big house and later became our gardener at the Lion. The end cottage is called Yew Tree and was occupied by Ben and Nancy Gwilt; Nancy used to work up at The Lion in the early fifties and did cups of tea and coffee from Yew Tree.

Before we bought the Lion in 1958 we had a weekend caravan behind The Lion from 1953. Ben Gwilt would let my father and me fish from the punt at the bottom of his garden. To the left of the road opposite the embankment was the dam wall of the upper holding dam, which was fed by means of the manmade canal.

There is another building close by which is said to be the company food store for the iron works, prior to that it had been used as stabling for the ironworkers' horses. The lane beside this house is now a studio for repairing stained glass windows, there is a lane which takes you up to the Old Smithy Mill. This was powered by a water race from the manmade canal and the smithy looked after the making and the maintenance of the iron parts used throughout the iron forge. When we arrived in the village this smithy cottage was occupied by Mr and Mrs Harold Partridge, he had only one good arm and one leg, his injuries came from the First World War, but they didn't stop him putting on his wooden leg to walk up the lane for forty Park Drive cigarettes every day. On one occasion Harold saw my mother using a Prestige can opener as since his wife had died and having only one arm he was unable to open any can, we were ordered to get one on our next visit to town and fit one in his cottage" (Whittle).

The Ferrymen: their dates and tales

The earliest recorded accident on the ferry dates back to 1607 and these two articles from *Transactions* tell the tale.

Disaster at Hampton Loade

The above article refers to a disaster at Hampton Loade where sixty eight people were drowned. I have looked through the parish register and found the entries concerning the disaster but find that it was in 1607 and not 1620 as stated. The register extracts make interesting reading as the burials were made over a period of several weeks, the river must have been reluctant to give up it's dead.

30 Nov 1607 Francis James and Robert Walles' wife of Fayntrey being two of them that were drowned were buried.

5 Dec 1607 The wife of John Hayward of Much Wenlock, being another of them which were drowned, was buried.

6 Dec 1607 Parnell, the wife of Humphrey Stringer of Fayntrey and Margaret the wife of John Harris of Deuxell and Elinor the wife of Thomas Fewtrell of Olbury were buried and were more of them which were drowned.

9 Dec 1607 Richard Acton of Bridgnorth, Ralphe Williams and his wife, strangers, John Parkes of Bridgnorth, John Jaxon of Bewdley, a young maid with a reed heade, whose name was not known, being drowned were buried.

12 Dec 1607 George Symons of Acton Rownde, Richard Clayton of Much Wenlock, and the wife of John Pearkes of Bridgnorth were buried, being more of them which were drowned.

16 Dec 1607 A stranger lade being drowned was buried.

1 Jan 1608 The wife of Thomas Smalman of Bridgnorth was buried and was one of the misse adventure.

8 Jan 1608 Francis Collins was buried and was one of them which were miss ventured.

Figure 6 **A disaster on the river in 1607.**

On 29th November 1620 there was, to use the quaint language of a contemporary diarist, "the greatest flood in ye river Severn that hath been since ye flood of Noah for there were drowned at Hamptones Loade sixty eight persons as they were going to Bewdley faire" (transactions, 1995, p111).

In 1871-1874 Thomas Porter is recorded as being the ferryman and in 1881 Henry Turley has taken the helm.

Figure 7 This postcard of the Unicorn Inn was posted in 1905 from Bridgnorth to West Kirby Cheshire complete with an old Severn trow complete with 'hut'. The picture was provided by Mr D.H. Dillon of Surrey.

The Bridgnorth Journal of Friday 24th January 2003 provides a glimpse of Hampton Loade life through the eyes of Joyce Cooper who reminisces about her child hood memories of the ferry and places several ferrymen in the time line of history.

Mr Thomas Bennett, was "the first man to go down the river when the ferry broke away midstream with a lady aboard, namely Mrs Mary Mottershead of Sutton Farm, Hampton Loade. It was at this time the iron boat (ferry) and was later recovered further down the river". Mr Bennett gave up the ferry in the late 1920s before moving to the other side of the river; he died on September 16th, 1946. 'The Iron boat' as it is described by Joyce was used by the local men for having a few beers and playing cards but the old boat was eventually lost to the war effort.

Figure 8 **Hampton Loade c 1944**
Mr Christie the ferrymen chats with Mrs Creed (no relation).
Mr Jimmy Christie took over the ferry from Mr Bennett and
stayed for about ten years leaving the ferry house in the late 1930s.
During this period the ferry has a below deck area, where locals
used to meet up to drink and play cards.

Figure 9 **A delightful picture of Hampton Loade Ferry**
taken by Mr Mottershead, the ferry man is Mr Christie and
the little girl is Jean Edmunds.

Mr Christie took over the ferry next and stayed about ten years in the late 1930s before going to live at the Bone Mill on the Dudmaston Estate. He served in the Royal Navy in the First World War and in 1940 he was called up once again for World War Two. He passed away on April 8, 1976 aged 80 after spending some time in Arden Way, Alveley, with his wife.

Mr Fred James and his wife Millie nee James ran the ferry for a very short time before returning to Highley where they had lived previously and handed the reigns over to a ferry lady by the name of Mrs Jacoba Daviers, she and her children came to Hampton Loade to escape the London Blitz.

In 1942 Mr Bill Parkes came from Smethwick to run the ferry for many years, he too went down the river with the ferry but lived to tell the tale, although it is said that he suffered after the events of the night of August 16th 1957. The hawser broke and he lost control and the ferry was swept away down the swollen river with William Parkes holding on to the mast. The terrifying ordeal in the dark on a fast moving river must have tested his courage but he managed to get to Arley in one piece where he was encouraged to jump off, which he did successfully. He continued to work on the river but it is said he was never the same jolly chap he once was.

The ferry then changed hands once again in 1958 when it went to Mr Gerald James the brother of previous owner, Fred James. Mr Gerald James and his daughter Mrs Annie Lillian James known affectionately as "Girlie" ran the ferry for many years, the later years aided by their son Robert. Gerald James

Figure 10 **The Ferry was relaunched in May 1958 and reappeared on the river proudly boasting a canopy.**

worked on the Great Western railway at Hampton Loade. He stayed in the background and it was "my mother who ran it", says Mrs Janet McAvoy, Girlie's daughter.

Janet nee James recalls the events of 1958 recorded in the Shropshire Star 1998. She is able to remember the relaunch event in the photograph and identifies herself as the girl at the front with her head half turned and her father Gerald James as the gentleman on the front to the right. Standing at the back of the boat is her brother Robert who drowned in 1964.

On December 13th 1964 tragedy struck when Gerald's and Girlie's son Robert and his cousin were managing the ferry, the details are unclear but it would appear that the ferry broke loose when a half submerged tree trunk struck underneath breaking the cable. The front dipped and Christopher Evans clung to the side of the ferry. The river was rising and flowing fast and as the ferry passed the cottages, it turned upside down. Gerald's son Robert jumped into the river to get help but was never seen again, he was just 22 years old.

Robert's mother, Annie remained in Hampton Loade to run the ferry with her sister Mrs Kathy Evans for many years, the tragedy not moving them from their home. The ladies used to be there in all weathers, responding to you ringing the bell attached to a piece of rope, activated on each side of the river, knowing that without the ferry the passenger or visitor could face a fourteen mile walk. Girlie said they didn't make a fortune from the ferry and charged ten pence each way but did it more for pleasure than profit, supplementing their income from selling eggs from their own chickens. The ferry was formerly used by the miners to and from Highley pit but it's now mainly for visitors.

In 1949 the fare rose to 3d each way and when Mr James took over he reduced it again, by 1983 it was ten pence each way and by 1995 it had doubled to twenty pence. The ferry served a long day and when operational still does, but long gone are the days when it started at 6 am to take the miners and railway workers to Highley. During the war German prisoners used the ferry to go and work on the farms on the west side of the river.

Today (2010) if we are fortunate to have it running at all, it costs seventy five pence each way. In 1939-45 children walked from Alveley to catch the train over the other side of the river to take them to school in Bridgnorth. Can you imagine how parents today would feel at funding the river and the rail fares?

Girlie and Kathy who were both born at The Unicorn Inn sold the ferry to Darren Page in February 1996 and 1998 "Girlie" Annie Lillian James died after running the ferry with her sister for nearly forty years.

Figure 11 **Girlie James and Kathy Evans, who ran the ferry for many years.**

The Ferry's historic chequered past has continued to cause more than a ripple in the water at Hampton Loade. Problems with the river and flooding have continued, by not only taking its passengers across the river but for an unfortunate few, along with it down the river! We must never forget the power of water and hold our nostalgic view of the river delights carefully beside our respect for the force it wields.

Once again problems with flooding created financial problems for the owner and the ferry remained out of action for several years. After a turbulent time of uncertainty both on the water and off, the new ferry project was completed on January 12th 2004 thanks to a grant of £17,000 from The Countryside Agency. A four hundred year old tree was shipped from France to Shropshire specifically for the new ferry in 2003. The new craft weighs 3-4 tonnes and measures 20ft by 9ft. It has been constructed from larch, with an oak frame; the hull of the boat has been covered with pitch, for added protection, so with luck the ferry should last just as long if not longer than previous models which have seen up to 38 years service.

In June 2007, the village on the west bank suffered major damage as a result of a severe rainstorm. The one and only road into the village was washed away. This affected services on the Severn Valley Railway, with a consequent loss of tourist revenue to the ferry and the local area. The Ferry remained closed until Friday 17th April 2009 when the newly formed Hampton Loade Community Trust (HLCT) succeeded in returning the Ferry back to the water. HLCT is a community interest company; a not for profit organisation and relies upon the drive and enthusiasm of its trustees, supporters and volunteers. HLCT has assumed responsibility for the operation and preservation of the ferry for the foreseeable future.

On Saturday 25th April 2009, the ferry carried its first passengers in nearly 2 years, across the River Severn by a group of enthusiastic support volunteers, but from the spring of 2010 has returned to the previous owner Darren Page. Let's hope this historic passage across the river has earned its right of stay and remains open for future generations.

Figure 12 **Hampton Loade Ferry, The Unicorn is in the background. Courtesy of Alveley Historical Society.**

Figure 13 **A lorry stuck while crossing the ford at Hampton Loade. Courtesy of Alveley Historical Society.**

Sid and Joyce Link's memories:

Figure 14

Lye Hall Farm, Hampton Loade.

"My brother and I were born in Hampton Loade, my brother was born in March and I was born in February and on both occasions the river was in flood. The midwife came from the other side of the river, she had to punt over as the ferry wasn't working, and my mother said she kept her eyes closed all the way over in fear. My father was a miner in Alveley and Kinlet and my mother went to school in Quatt. I lived most of my life in Hampton Loade I remember as a lad there was an overhead pulley going over the river which pulled damsons and other fruits to go on the train to Manchester.

I remained there after my marriage in 1953. My wife and I lived in the village for many years, we did several things at one time we kept a few thousand chickens, but the river made it difficult. Each time the river flooded we raised the chicken sheds up in stilts, but each time the river would follow. On one occasion Jim Mottershed from Lye Hall farm came down in his tractor and helped me move the chickens out of danger, they were then collected and sold; we couldn't cope with the flooding.

Our house was a mission hall originally, it was just four stone walls and a roof when we bought it, we had to make it into a cottage and a home as it was less than basic. We bought it off Mr Stewart Morley Tonkin a publisher who had been using it as storage for his books etc. While we waited for the cottage to be finished we lived in a caravan on the Unicorn land on the other side of the river. When we finished a man from the council came and he stood in the bedroom deciding whether to pass it or not and he told us it was not regulation height, it was four inches too low, so he told us to raise the roof. I took some advice from someone on the housing committee and he told us to just move in so we did and nothing ever happened. We later received a letter from the House of Commons telling us that the laws had been relaxed and it was all cleared up. We built a cafe, Links cafe in 1964 and sold it to a lady who ran it for a very short time before David Browning of The River and Rail, purchased it from her in the 1970s. We left our home 'Linwood', which is a combination of our surnames Lin from Link and wood from Woodhouse, in 1971. We did later try to buy it back again but we just missed it".

An interview with David Browning, owner of the River and Rail Public house.

"I first came to Hampton Loade in 1975 when a friend of mine Roy Columbel brought me down to show me two almost derelict cottages he had just purchased in the Hamlet for £3,000, Roy knocked these two cottages into one which was a great success. I then started helping him to renovate them at weekend and holidays, we got on really well and I enjoyed the work and loved the village. The neighbours at that time were Ben and Nancy Gwilt, Bert Pitt and his wife and then in the end cottage was Claire, Bill's widow, Bill used to work on the ferry.

Figure 15 **A very rare picture of the front of the cottages, painted in oil, artist and year unknown.**

Although it was only a tiny hamlet it was quite a busy place, The Lion public house created a lot of traffic as it was a very busy destination pub, people came from all over the place to go there, there were fishermen from up and down the river, walkers, the residents from the caravan site and people visiting the Hampton Loade station so although it quite a tranquil place it was busy at times. It never detracted from the ambience of the village though and when I noticed that the little café and a three bed roomed house was for sale I didn't need much persuasion to put an offer in as I loved the place and I was delighted when it was accepted. I bought the café and house for £20,000, the café was an old wooden austere place, functional for the needs at the time I suppose, but Cathy and I (my wife to be at the time), made a few changes. We turned it into an afternoon tea shop and ran if for three seasons whilst getting planning permission for something a bit bigger as we wanted to open a restaurant."

The Haywain Years
by David Browning

"*The Haywain Restaurant* at Hampton Loade was opened in 1981 after years of planning, building, purchasing, preparation and sheer hard work. By the time we opened we also had two daughters, Mellissa and Juliet, who stayed here until they went to University and moved away. We bought two donkeys Jacob and Bobbie in 1978; they lived in a shed in the paddock which my architect Roy Duckworth built, the shed has since been turned into a wood shed but the paddock is now the beer garden. The children visiting the restaurant loved to feed the donkeys scraps of food and carrots etc whilst the parents relaxed in the restaurant, it was a good arrangement.

Figure 16 **Cathy and David Browning, the proud owners of**
The Haywain Restaurant c 1980.

The Mottershed's ran the National Trust car park when I first moved here, as well as the farm which had been in the family for over a century.

They opened the car park in all weathers sitting in a little wooden hut from dawn to dusk; they kept the bins clear, cleaned the two toilets and made sure it was all in order, charging just 10p per car per day. They have moved away now and the car park is automated with no toilets and no one on duty anymore and it costs one pound per day now.

I later purchased another piece of land from Sid Link, which was once part of the old reservoir and another piece from the National Trust on the river front, I shared the cost and land with Colin Ellingham, my neighbour".

The Haywain Restaurant became one of the most respected and popular restaurants in Shropshire, we won many accolades including: The AA Guide, The Michelin guide, and many others, we had top chefs working for us and celebrity customers, they were great years in the mid 1980s and it was good to be a part of it.

"We decided to change to a pub after the economics in the country began to alter, we needed to change to survive, and when The Lion decided to close we considered our options and made the decision to close the gourmet restaurant and open a public house.

We changed the name to the *River and Rail* and now we serve people all day in all weathers. People love to come out to the country and enjoy the peace and tranquillity we have here".

The celebrity visitors and entrepreneurs who visited the Haywain:

"When Richard Branson came to Shropshire to secure the purchasing of the Telford Balloon Company he came in here afterwards for a meal.
Robert Plant, Status Quo and Snooker players, Bill Werbeniuk, Rex Williams and Joe Davis".

Figure 17 **Inside The Haywain Restaurant, 1980s.**

Figure 18 **The Haywain Restaurant.**

The Lion Inn

The Lion joined the vanishing Inns of Shrewsbury in 2009

Figure 19 The Lion Inn, now a row of cottages, you can still just see the old public house sign in the centre. It began life as a beer house providing refreshments to the iron workers along the lane.

Figure 20 An aerial view of The Lion.

"The King of the beasts is well represented on British pub signs both in its natural state and those occurring in heraldry. The most obvious intention of the families using such a devise is to associate themselves with The Lion's courage and strength" (Rose.p6).

The Old Lion was built around 1570, stood at the end of the lane close to the Iron works. The exterior of the cottage remains largely untouched from when it was built during the industrial revolution, by men who replaced their sickle with a smelting iron.

The Parish records for Chelmarsh (mentioned in the doomsday book as Chelmeres) reveal that there were two brothers by the name of Albert and Tom Abbott who ran a mobile cider press from Hampton Loade, making cider for the surrounding villages. Excess apples could be packed off on the train at Hampton Loade and sent to Manchester for use as dye in the cotton trades. It is humble beginnings such as these that could have laid the foundation stones for the Brew house.

An ale house was a place where intoxicants, as deemed proper by the innkeeper were to be drunk on the premises 'where sold', which is pertinent here as we understand the beer to be given in part payment of the wages for the workers at the iron works. Licensing initially began in 1495, and the Alehouse Act in 1552 required all victuallers and alehouse keepers to be licensed by the Justices. There are no records here for the beer house it replaced as it was a private beerhouse until 1831. We only have the church records to reveal snippets of information as to the occupation of some of the hamlet's inhabitants.

The Duke of Wellington's controversial Beer House act of 1830 altered the way in which beer was sold. It was called The Duke of Wellington Act because it was passed whilst the Duke was Prime Minister. The Beer houses Act was a means of diverting the poor from gin or rum, which was a huge problem at the time. The act allowed anyone – on payment of a fee of two guineas to the local excise authorities – to sell beer but not wine or spirits without a licence, in contrast to a licensed victualler who could sell all types of drink and required a licence from local magistrates. This led to a marked increase in the number of public houses for the consumption of beer only– and there became about 30,000 establishments throughout Britain as a result. It is at this juncture that we have the first record for the brew house now referred to as 'The Lion Inn'.

Some beer houses had names, such as 'The Lion' whilst others were known by colloquial terms perhaps simply as the 'Forge house' or 'Hemptons house', which sometimes developed into the official registration name. There are several given reasons as to why the beer houses or Inns developed names and swinging signs, one accepted theory is because very few people could read, and therefore a sign was necessary.

Only a short while later, The Beer House Act of 1834 draws a distinction between houses for the retailing of beer to be drunk on or off the premises which were to be known as beer houses and beer shops, where the beer was sold for consumption off the premises, The Wine and Beer Act of 1869 placed them all on an equal footing.

In 1872, there were 42,590 beer houses in England and Wales, but none in Scotland or Ireland, and there were 3,162 licences issued to people who sell beer for consumption *off* the premises. Beer houses eventually disappeared and were replaced by licensed victuallers.

A list of all the owners / licensees of The Lion Inn

The Holloway family are recorded as living at Hampton Loade in **1831**; William Holloway a Cooper (barrel maker) which was his main source of income lived on site at The Lion. It was not uncommon for beer house-keepers to have another trade or business to supplement their income as was the case here. He is listed with his wife Ann and children William Junior, Henry and Ann Wright a lady of 'independent means' which could be Ann's mother and a servant by the name of Mary Bennett. The family were still there in **1851** when Henry aged 17 had become a hoop maker for the barrels his father makes and Ann senior had reached the ripe old age of 85.

"Geology and terrain was a major factor for the Lion and the ferry being situated in the hamlet [...], it was the best river crossing between Bridgnorth and Bewdley. This made two livelihoods possible, the Inn catered for the weary traveller on the river and the road and in times of flood he would gain trade from people waiting to cross by ferry or ford. The ferry man had always made a good living, from as far back as history can go, but from the start of the industrial revolution, the craft using the river escalated in size and weight" [Whittle].

The licensing magistrates from Bridgnorth visited The Lion in 1896 and record the Holloways as still running the family business. Henry Holloway is Licensee Occupier and manager for the previous 23 years, replacing his father as licensee in 1863.

The land around the Lion was at one time standing at two and a half acres in 1896, but by 1901 they had sold off the land and reduced the annual rateable value from £14. 5s to £10.6s. The nature of the local trade by then was said to be agricultural and the condition of the establishment is recorded as 'good and clean' upon inspection which had by this time become a requirement under the new Wine and Spirit Beer house act of 1869 which required beer houses to apply for a licence from the magistrates.

In **1908** Mrs Emma Holloway was in situ, later to be assisted by Edwin Woodbeer in **1913**, who is listed as the beer retailer. Widow Emma is still the licensee, a position she held until 1915.

The Holloway family were licensees for at least 84 long years, (a record to be proud of) as records prior to that are nonexistent. It's difficult to say how many further generations of Holloways went back as brewers of The Lion or the brew house which it replaced but records do show two Holloway Brothers as renting gardens in the hamlet in 1622, is it coincidence that the names were Henry and William? After the Holloways there was Charles Shelley who was listed as the licensee in 1915 and still appears in Kelly's directory as the Beer retailer in 1947, a good run of over thirty years but not to the measure of the Holloways.

There then followed quite a few licensees in quick succession. It is rumoured that this is because the Holloways haunt the building, never malicious or frightening but just make their presence felt and occasionally seen. Perhaps the licensees couldn't cope with the 'spirits'.

1947-1949 Christopher Groves, owned by Reg Smith.
1949-1950 Agnes Groves
1950-1951 James C King
1951-1954 Walter H Pannell
1954-1955 Jack Fryer
1955-1958 Arnold Dunn
1958 John Mathews

Then begins the three generations of Whittles who owned the Lion from November 1958 for 45 years, the last owner occupying a cottage on that site, where a plaque with this lament to its past is proudly displayed on the old white washed walls for all to see.

Vic and Betty Whittle departed life at the Lion in 1976 and 1999 respectively and the last family of Whittles ran the pub until it finally called last orders for the final time on 13th April 2003.

The Lion public house was renowned for its country wines and was in the good pub guide in 2003 and AA guide 2003. The country wines can now be purchased at The River and Rail public house which remains in the village.

Figure 21 **An old Lion Label for County Wines.**

A Lion's last lament
All ghosts now

How is it possible to define a ghost?
Perhaps it is the presence of the host.

I see a row of three cottages for all their sins
Where once I saw one of England's finest Inns.

The Inn is long gone from the end of the road
Three families now live in that spacious abode.

I Wonder is the shadowing grey full figure of George in full lament,
Does he still haunt the hostelries original rooms with no repent?

As I look through the old bar window
It has changed so little, who is that sitting by the yawning fireplace, could it be a Whittle?

Some do not want to believe what they can't understand and see; its surely
Mary and Jon in the new gardens under that tree.

I sense Rob's presence looking out at his pretty serving wenches, as they politely tend to the lawn customers at their benches.
Are these just my fading memories or
Are they really ghosts? I cannot say,
But to me they'll always be the finest hosts.

By Rob Whittle

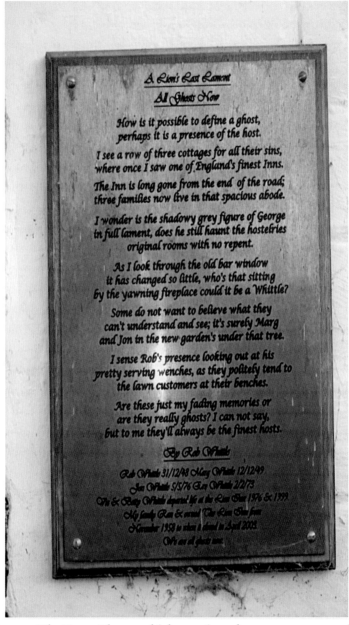

Figure 22 **The Brass Plaque which remains where once an open sign would have hung.**

The Hamlet's very own Iron Bridge, local folklore tells us that the little rather unimpressive looking bridge along the lane towards The Lion was a prototype for The Iron Bridge in Coalbrookdale, the first cast-iron bridge to be

constructed in Europe. There may be some merit in the locals' belief that the bridge plays an important part in Shropshire history during the industrial revolution. It is undeniable that it is important to the history of Hampton Loade and there appears to be a growing strength of feeling that it is more important than has been previously considered. However, as always, proof is required and there appears to be no obvious signs in the design that this local bridge should predetermine the finished result of the Ironbridge. On the other hand, as design technology and engineering is a science unfamiliar to the lay man, it warrants more than just a speculative glance, some contextual research proved to be essential here. The history of local iron making, the experimental work with iron being done locally, iron works in the hamlet and the bridge itself appeared to be the most obvious place to start.

It was clearly evident that any association between the two bridges would be difficult to prove as the little bridge has lost much of its associate history and has undergone alterations in recent years. It may be not ever be possible to determine just how important it once was, but there are be some clues determining just why its local status receives such merit.

The Iron Bridge at Coalbrookdale

The Iron Bridge in Shropshire was designed by the architect Thomas Pritchard, using carpentry-style joints and built by the iron-master Abraham Darby.

Darby's cast-iron works were the site of important improvements in iron smelting technology which alongside other developments, led to the Industrial Revolution in England. The bridge was originally used to transport iron, coal, and limestone across the river. Despite its pioneering technology in 1779, as the first structural use of cast iron, no eye witness accounts are known which describe the Iron Bridge being erected.

We now know that all the large castings were made individually as they are all slightly different. The joints would all be familiar to a carpenter – mortise and tenons, dovetails and wedges – this was the traditional way in which iron structures were joined at the time. The builders did use timber fixing techniques, but there are also over 200 nut and bolt fixings. At the time these were not widely used, so the bridge shows a migration from joinery-driven fixing to engineering-driven techniques: no one had attempted anything like this before.

Figure 23 **Picture of the Bridge 2009 by Omar Aguao.**

The Iron Bridge at Hampton Loade

Figure 24 Ironbridge, Oct 2009.
Beginning date of construction 1775, Completion date, 1779 and opened on 1st January 1781.

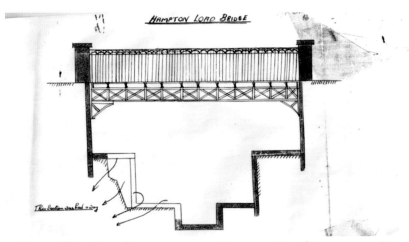

Figure 25 The plans for a new top on Hampton Loade's very own iron bridge after vehicle damage.

In Comparison

It certainly is a very old little bridge and is sited within smelting distance of the old iron works. Some local residents remember the tale of it being floated along the river to arrive at Hampton Loade, which could eliminate the myth that it may have been made in the Hamlet.

The cast iron bridge is made in three foot sections and is dove tailed together as practised in the carpentry trade. It now carries a narrow private road over a sluice opening, once forming part of the water management system from 1786 when a forge was established at Hampton Loade by William Whitmore and permission was granted to erect two dams to serve the works. This suggests that the bridge may therefore date to sometime c1786. The northern approach to the bridge is along the dam embankment and it is possible that access to the village was once made by this route. Both ends of the bridge are denoted by a pair of brick pillars, topped by shallow triangular stone finials. The bridge balustrade is formed by modern square section iron railings topped by a rail, which replaced the original railings lost to an accident

Figure 26 **View from underneath the Iron Bridge. It has a unique beam structure under the base and recent photographs taken from under the bridge by Omar Aguao in 2009 reveal the structure in spite of the plentiful foliage surrounding it.**

in 1970s. Attached to the outer side of the balustrade are a series of wrought iron decorative embellishments.

In 1972 two accidents involving a car and later a van destroyed the top of this historic bridge which was shattered into pieces, it was replaced not by cast iron as cost prohibited, but by a top made in box section steel. The survival of the bridge enabled a closer inspection of the technical details of the bridge.

These 's' shaped supports are the vestiges of the original cast iron top of the bridge. They are cruder 's' shapes than those on The Ironbridge and over time the weather has taken its toll to the extent that they have been damaged and snapped. There is no charitable trust to support their upkeep; they are therefore currently broken and unpainted.

Figure 27 **The decorative embellishments on the Hampton Loade bridge.**

A request for listing with English Heritage

In 2006 a request to consider listing the cast iron bridge at Hampton Loade was submitted to The National Heritage Trust in response to concerns that increasing use of the bridge by heavy vehicles may result in it being damaged and/or replaced. The bridge, although privately owned, is the only access route for 26 residences. The Trust examined the bridge and found no date on any part of it and concluded as we did that there was no way of determining the exact date of the bridge. This lack of dating coupled by the fact that the railings on the top were modern replacements resulted in the Trust's understandable decision not to list the bridge as "given the degree of alteration, including the loss of its original balustrade, it does not therefore meet the standards for listing in a national context. The heritage context of the bridge has also been somewhat compromised by the removal of many buildings and structures associated with the forge and it consequently does not have group value which might otherwise raise its interest" (Heritage).

The Heritage report describes the bridge as "an example of an unusual form of the simple beam type [...] which is small and unimpressive, (and it) is probably a late example of a failed design form, [...] erected in the 1840s-1850s or even later using engineering which was already becoming outdated." Whilst it is true that it is a very unimpressive bridge in itself, the question of why anyone would put in place a bridge of a failed design form using out dated engineering is intriguing, unless of course it was not yet proven to be a failing design form when erected, which may date it to closer to the creation of the iron works.

Unfortunately, the forge area is not depicted on any early estate maps and is blank on the Tithe Apportionment Map of 1849. The area is first depicted on the 1883/4 Ordnance Survey Map on which the forge buildings are shown, but the complex is described as disused. The mapping also notes the presence of a weir, but does not clearly show the bridge although it probably did exist by this time as the form of the surviving structure suggests a mid C19 date (English Heritage). The report does state that the bridge whilst unimpressive is atypical;

"The cast iron lattice girder bridge structure is of the simple beam type supported at either end by brick parapets. Cast iron bridges of this type of construction are known to be inherently weak and this in part may explain why few examples survive. There are no other listed bridges with this form of lattice girder. An extensive search through published images of iron bridges similarly failed to reveal any examples of this particular form of design and consultation with a leading expert in cast iron bridges confirmed that this form of bridge is uncommon. Dating of the bridge is crucial to understanding its importance. The dam and sluice of which it forms a part is known to date to 1786 and if this bridge was built at this time it would represent an early example representing an innovative design" (English Heritage).

So, do we have 'cast iron' proof that the Bridge was a prototype for the Iron Bridge? No, clearly the dating would suggest not, but the case remains open as yet.

Further research reveals that the Hamlet once played host to a very famous engineer, one John Urpeth Rastrick and question whether the bridge was the reason for his presence. Rastrick was a mechanical and civil engineer who constructed several early steam railway locomotives. He kept a diary which is reproduced for us in Mutton's work in which he mentions his visit of 1806.

An account of Rastrick's visit to Hampton Loade

Taken from the diary of John Urpeth Rastrick
Journal of my own time

"On 5th May 1806 Rastrick had been to Mr. Vernon's house at Wolver-hampton and agreed to visit Vernon's brother at Hampton Loade, and after dinner at two o'clock we set off for the Heath Forge [in Staffordshire] and got there about three o'clock. We stopped there about half an hour and then made to Hampton Loade. There Mr. Thos. Vernon has the management of an iron work. We found him and his wife at home; the works consist of a tilt forge, and pair of puddling Rolls worked by a water wheel which takes the water at the top, two puddling furnaces at the upper work. The lower works are drove by a water wheel 20 feet dia, and ten foot wide works a pair of Shingling and Bar Rolls, and one Pair of Boiler Plate Rolls, one pair of large shears and one pair of small shears, (Two heating Furnaces).

We got there by tea time and found it a very pleasant situation close by the River Severn. There is also another mill above the upper work drove by a water wheel for turning the rolls, but meant for blowing of a Finery. We spent the evening very agreeably, and went to bed about twelve o'clock.

6th May When I got up this morning I found Mr. Thos Vernon and Mr. Vernon up and out. I followed them and went up the Brook where the water comes to the mill thro' a wood by the side of a hill we saw a quarry for making of paper (brown). Came back again and went thro' the works and saw the Mill go, and about twelve o'clock we left there for Bridgnorth, and after a ride of about an hour and half arrived at the hand and bottle Inn where we dined. After dinner we went to Mr. Hazeldine and Co. Foundery (sic) but he was not there. We went over to his house and found he had just set off for the foundery. We returned and found him, he showed us through the works, and then we went over to the town and at a publick-house (sic) we had a great deal of conversation and after some little explanation Mr. Hazeldine and I proposed to join in partnership and he told me his proposals which were to take an equal share in the business with him and do all the outdoor work and attend to the putting up the machinery. I told him I would come to a conclusion as soon as possible […] we went to the Hand and Bottle…"

Rastrick stayed in partnership with Hazeldine until 1817 at the Bridgnorth Foundry. In 1819 he joined James Foster in partnership at the Stourbridge Ironworks and stayed there until 1831, by which time he was well known as one of the early railway engineers (Mutton).

* * * * *

The confirmation of his presence does little to establish a date for the bridge or his connection to it, the diary does however place his significant interest in what was happening at the iron works to recount it in his diary. Rastrick forms a link from his own interests in Hampton Loade to the Ketley iron works where his father was a manager. Ketley's carries its own prominence with a host of now famous industrial associates; names now synonymous with the engineering feats and pioneering works such as; the Darby's, Thomas Telford, Reynolds and Rastrick.

The importance of Ketley's cannot be understated here, The Ketley iron works were leased out in 1715 from Lord Gower, to Richard Hartshorne of Ketley, master collier, for 21 years. Hartshorne died in 1733 and his widow Jane held the lease at her death in 1737. In 1754 Abraham Darby (II) became the lessee; and soon afterwards the Ketley ironworks began production.

Abraham Darby is a name known to all of us as the name behind the Ironbridge, however, as there were four Abraham Darby's its pertinent to understand that each one of these Quaker ironmasters played a part to a greater or lesser degree towards the industrial revolution. Collectively they were responsible for a series of technological changes with regard to the making of iron. Abraham Darby I took lease upon a deserted iron foundry in Coalbrookdale. The site was an ideal location; he only had to repair the existing furnace which was driven by water power from the River Severn. It was not until 1738 that Abraham Darby II became a partner in the company. His major contribution was in making forgeable iron in 1748, the company was controlled until 1771 by Richard Reynolds, (see the forges chart of 1790) he was son-in-law of Darby II and a Quaker. The Coalbrookdale Company continued to expand and offices were opened in Liverpool, Bridgnorth and organisations of agents were established throughout the country: by 1777 Darby's son-in-law Richard Reynolds was now the lessee. In that year Reynolds's Ketley mines produced 20,733 tons of Clod coal for coking and 2,741 tons of other coals. Reynolds seems to have passed his interest in the ironworks, to his sons William and Joseph around 1789 and the lease was renewed to them in 1797.

Darby III was a more adventurous ironmaster. He believed that there was nothing that could not be made from iron and in order to prove his faith in the product he supported the idea for a bridge over the Severn Gorge. In 1777 through the death of T. F. Pritchard, the original architect, he was left with the ultimate supervision of the design and construction of the Iron Bridge. In 1789 Abraham Darby III died and his grandsons Abraham Darby IV and Alfred Darby entered the company in the 1820's. They embarked on a programme of reform as the company's fortunes had slumped following the Napoleonic War boom. They were also responsible for the Coalbrookdale Company's success at the Great Exhibition at Crystal Palace in 1851.

If we pay any heed to our oral history and seek an association between *The Ironbridge* and this little old local one the, then this family link may the clue. We know a lot of iron testing and casting work was made for Thomas Telford, at the Ketley iron works, Telford was experimenting with iron tubs ready for canal work resulting in his design and production of an iron aqueduct (Trinder.94).

John, Urpeth, Rastrick, engineer and the Ketley iron works

John Rastrick was born on 26th January 1770 in Morpeth, son to John senior who was an engineer at the Ketley ironworks from Oakengates, and Mary (nee Urpeth) Rastrick.

Rastrick was a mechanical and civil engineer who constructed several early steam railway locomotives.

In around 1807/8 he joined John Hazeldine of Bridgnorth – a foundry business where he was involved with Trevithick engines including *Catch Me Who Can* which was demonstrated in London in autumn 1808 on a circular demonstration circuit near what is now Euston Square. It was built at the Hazeldine foundry at Bridgnorth, Shropshire and weighed eight tons. In about 1817, after Hazeldine's death, Rastrick became managing partner of Bradley, Foster, Rastrick & Co. of Stourbridge, Worcestershire. This firm produced much ironwork for buildings, including the British Museum, the General Post Office in London and the Long Room of Customs House. He retained his autonomy and was engineer to the Stratford and Moreton Railway in 1822 which used continuous wrought iron rail.

He was responsible for the manufacture of many kinds of machinery and developed a special interest in railway construction. He was engineer for the

Stratford-upon-Avon and Moreton-in-Marsh Railway in 1822 and gave evidence in support of the Liverpool & Manchester Railway Bill in 1826. In 1828 he designed the locomotive 'The Agenoria' for the Shutt End Railway, near Stourbridge, and built three similar locomotives the following year for the Delaware and Hudson Railroad in the USA. One of these, 'Stourbridge Lion', was the first steam railway locomotive to run in North America. In 1828 Horatio Allen, agent of the Delaware & Hudson Canal Co., ordered the

Stourbridge Lion from Foster Rastrick and *Agenoria* was a similar locomotive constructed for the Shutt End Railway in 1829. Agenoria is now on display at the National Railway museum in York.

Rastrick was involved in the Grand Junction Railway and was engineer-in-chief

Figure 28 **Agenoria.**

of the London & Brighton Railway where his works included the notable Ouse Valley Viaduct and the Preston Road Viaduct which survived severe bomb damage in World War two. He retired from active life in 1847, moving to Sayes Court, Addlestone, Chertsey in Surrey with 25 acres of ground. He joined the Institution of Civil Engineers in 1827, became a Fellow of the Royal Society on 19 January 1837. He died at Sayes Court in Surrey on 1 November 1856 and is buried in Brighton, his notebooks are preserved at the Science Museum.

If John Urpeth Rastrick was involved with the erection of the bridge then it was built as suspected by English Heritage much later than the Ironbridge at Coalbrookdale. However, there is just one more avenue of research to follow, that of the old iron works, some more recent findings revealed by David Poyner predate the previous research undertaken by English Heritage and further add speculation to the conjecture.

The old Ironworks at Hampton Loade

This chapter draws on three vital resources to build up a contextual view of Hampton Loade's old ironworks.

The first is an extract of work originally produced by Norman Mutton on the forges of Hampton Loade, which forms part of a wider study on charcoal iron making, highlighting the ownership and activities of the ironworks.

Secondly, the studies by David Poyner, one on the forge at Top Mill and the other on the furnaces of Hampton Loade, some of which are reproduced in The Alveley *Transactions* 2000 and finally Richard Hyman's thesis of 2003 is the final article which reveals a third mill and a network of tunnels in the hamlet which was once part of the iron works.

The works at Hampton Loade were at the convergence of Paper Mill Brook and the River Severn. In the mid 17th century a blast furnace was operated at Hampton Loade and operated by the Midland iron-master, Thomas Foley, the son of a Dudley nail maker. The family business largely revolved around the production of bar iron and pig iron, this trade made much use of river transport and warehouses.

> "The first references to Hampton Loade Furnace come in the 1640s. In 1623 Thomas Gervois granted Lye Hall in Quatt to Richard Nash, Margaret his wife and Mary their daughter. In 1647 there was a settlement on behalf of Margaret for £42-10.00d pa between Richard Nash on one part and Seabright Nash and Thomas Beardsmore of the other part. This document indicates that the lands included in the original 1623 lease now included portions sublet to Richard Edwards, Walter Blunt and also 'one furnace known as Hampton Loade furnace in the holding of Thomas Foley'" (Poyner.2009).

The Lye Hall estate forms the boundary between Quatt and Alveley, just north of the present Paper Mill Brook. This strongly suggests that the furnace was roughly on the site later occupied by Hampton Loade Forge. The furnace had been in existence for several years by the time of the 1647 document, for on 13th April 1641 Thomas Foley reached an agreement with John Heath of

Alveley, a miller, Heath held a mill known as Elliot's or Moorhouse Mill. Foley had built a dam across the stream below his mill, to divert it to his furnace. The dam had raised the stream above its normal height, causing damage to the mill. Foley agreed to pay Heath £1-6-8d pa for seven years to indemnify him against claims for damages by Launcelot Lee, the mill owner" (Poyner.2000).

In 1653 Thomas Whitmore has business dealings with the works at Hampton Loade and by 1786, William Whitmore, who by now owned the land on the Quatt bank of the brook, was given permission to construct a dam across the brook and divert the water. Works started on the development of a forge at the site, the works were split into two sites; the smaller of the two was part of Hill House within the manor of Alveley.

Any remains of the furnace would now be buried beneath the 18/19th century forge, but it is possible that the water management system of the later forge reused that constructed for the furnace. Foley appears to have abandoned the site in 1662. The forge was leased to William Jones, a Stourbridge ironmaster and by 1790 became a small specialised charcoal forge, producing high quality wrought iron.

Abstract of Title

In an Abstract of Title on the 28th April 1796, of the assignees of William Bates and William Jones from Mr. John Hinksman the executors of John Hazeldene and the trustee of Robert Thompson to leasehold the ironworks at Hamptons Loade.

Bates and Jones later sold off part of the land around the works in 1812 which included Furnace Bank, the slang under the coppice, the little meadow and the forge pool with liberty to make dams' weir and pools although no buildings were to be erected within 200 yards of the local paper mill. They also sold "the leasehold land and tenements and dwelling house adjoining or being near to the ferry at Hampton Loade including the ferry, rafts and landing places, from William Whitmore of Dudmaston who leases the paper brook, the forge and the ferry to Thompson in 1801, who later sold it off again in 1832 to Henry Bradley (Mutton).

In 1796 Edward Oakley leased just over an acre to John Thompson later of Lye Hall, a prominent iron master of Colborne Hill, Old Swinford. He established the Hwycoed blast furnaces; these were blown by water powered machinery constructed at the Bridgnorth Foundry of John Hazeldine.

Hazeldine was the brother of William Hazeldine the Shrewsbury iron master and supplier of castings to Thomas Telford. Poyner suggests that John Thompson s castings at the forge were provided by Hazeldine when it was first equipped.

Thompson later leased the larger plot of land approximately six acres for 21 years at £45 per year along with Lye Hall farm, Paper Brook, the ferry and the forge and in 1797 began making fine iron in Hampton Loade by 1819 it was a small puddling works of only 3 furnaces employing 20 men. He operated forges at this time in both Hampton Loade and Eardington. It was Thompson who built the forge mill, engine, furnaces, the buildings for the iron making and two cottages. The two furnaces were each 40ft high, blown by waterwheel machinery constructed at Hazeldine's Foundry at Bridgnorth for £12 a ton. The wheel worked until 1875 when the works closed (Mutton).

Later reorganisation in 1819 associated with a change of ownership which resulted in both sites of the works being sold by the end of 1819 to W.O. Foster who was in control of both the forge sites. James Foster, his nephew and successor later became the sole owner of the work, he manufactured bar iron and iron goods and machines at the large works of John Bradley and Co. at Stourbridge and the adjoining works of Foster, Rastrick and Co, with smaller works at Shutt end, Eardington and Hampton Loade (Mutton). This period of time from 1819-1826 was one of the most interesting periods but Foster deemed it as a commercial disappointment. In spite of an ever deepening

Figure 29 **The walls of the old forge 2010.**

depression James Foster was expanding his interests and engaging in technical experiments. Within a few months of Foster taking over, the works were enlarged to J.U. Rastricks designs. There was work on a new wharf, two new rolls put in place and two new puddling furnaces were built.

In August 1820 it must have been an exceptionally hot month as the records show that the puddlers were given an extra 5 shillings worth of ale in consequence of suffering from extreme heat, the men would have supped their ale at The Lion Inn along the lane.

The Forges c.1790

Name		Forges					Mills
finery	*chafery*	*melting fineries*	*balling furnaces*	*built*	*rolling mill*	*slitting mills*	*built*
Ketley	R Reynolds & Co	2	6	1786	1	1	1787
Donnington Wood	W Reynolds & Co		4	1786			
Cleobury Dale	Botfield & Co		2		1	1	
Prescott	Botfield & Co						
Upton	Wheeler & Co		3		1		
Norton	Wheeler & Co		2		1		
Eardington	Wheeler & Co	3	2		2	1	
Wytheford	J Dorset		2		1		
Uffington	Wheeler & Co		1				
Caynton	Hallen		2		1		
Sambrook	Hallen		1		1		
Tibberton	Hallen		1				
Longnor	W Jones		2				
Pitchford	Lawrence & Hazeldine		1		1		
Lizard	Lawrence & Hazeldine		1		1		
Rock Mills	Dale Co						
Wrens Nest	Wright & Jesson	1	2			2	
Cleobury	Sir W Blount		3			2	
Hampton Loade	**William Jones**		1				

Figure 30 **Forges and Mills in Shropshire c1790. Source: B&W MII/5/10. The entry for Ketley shows six melting fineries for making stamped iron, which probably denote two each at Ketley, Horsehay and Coalbrookdale. But the major casualty of the depression was one of the larger works, Ketley, which was closed and then sold in 1818 by Joseph Reynolds, brother of the late William Reynolds.**

A group of workmen are pictured digging out slag at the old ironworks at Hampton Loade. Society member and chairman of Highley (history society Initiative David Poyner has written a chapter about Hampton Loade furnaces in the latest edition of Alveley Transactions. This old photograph is taken from the Historical society's *Images of Alveley* publication, which was released this year.

Richard Hayman's thesis of 2003 looks at the importance of Shropshire iron making. In it he includes this old chart which reveals the Mills and Forges with the occupiers. The date of the survey is uncertain, but Hayman had dated it by the occupation of the companies which are documented and arrived at the approximate date of c1790 for the survey. He also mentions Hampton Loade specifically as:

> "the only Severn Valley forge that was not associated with stamping and potting. In 1796 it was acquired by John Thompson, who apparently enlarged the works, but was superseded in 1803 by the Hampton Loade Iron Company. The forge remained a customer for Old Park pig iron until 1804 and continued in production after it was purchased by James Foster in 1820" (Hayman).

ℋampton ℒoade Forge

*Oh to see Hampton Loade's old forge in its prime, with huge dams
And water wheels, oh to be a traveler in time.
An orange halo and sparks light up the whole night sky, five
Furnaces heat fluid iron to a whit glow in a sulphurous pie.
What a feat to build this technical and powerful forge, with muscle
And sweat from the brow of long dead men like Sam and George.
A mighty dam holds back a huge lake and the Paper Mill Brook, it
Powered wheels, bellows and heavy hammers that broke off the
Impurities as they struck.*

*Barges and Trowes moor the wharf after a long watery journey so
slow, cargoes of pig iron, peat and charcoal, will make a molten river flow.
The puddlers and their lads mind the hot furnaces day and night, their only
solace strong ale to keep them cool throughout their light.
Tis all gone no the forge has seen its Waterloo, no need for fine iron ingots no
need for a crew.
In Hampton Loade the Great Western does crow, you will never see
Another barge or Severn Trowe.
Redundant great houses, dams with Sluices and waterfalls, leave cold
echoes around empty courtyards and roofless walls.*

*All reborn again as the splendid forge falls,
A tasteful home and garden within the foundry walls.*

By Rob Whittle

Between June and November 1822 a tin works designed by J.U. Rastrick was built on the site for rolling and tinning charcoal in sheets; it is noteworthy as being the site of the only tinplate works in Shropshire and was built during a difficult economic period. In spite of Fosters best efforts the tin plate works ceased production in the summer of 1826. He returned to the production of pig iron from charcoal and by 1830 the procedure had changed to the production of 'stewed charcoal' and he experimented with peat as fuel in the finery forges in the 1830 and 1840s. However, even by the 1830 good quality iron making was suffering the effects of recession and the forge closed for good in 1866. There is very little documented activity for the forge from that period, all that is recorded notes that the latter years produced horse nails and it took until 1900 before the stocks of machinery were disposed of and buildings demolished. It is recorded that the rector of Quatt purchased some of the blue bricks from the derelict buildings.

There is very little that survives from this era other than the walls, the bridge, the echoes of the men and the gushing water wheels on a very calm day. However David Poyner discovered a little more about the water mills associated with the forge and recalls his visit of May of 1999 when he and other members of the Alveley Historical Society visited the site and were shown a tunnel. Intrigued by its very existence Poyner returned in June of the same year with permission from the land owners for a second time. The top mill or upper mill could very well have been the one mentioned by Rastrick in 1806. Poyner notes that;

"Much evidence of the management of the water at the forge site survives. The 1786 dam and leat for the upper pool remain; the dam is built of blocks of the local sandstone and is about 20 feet high. The sluice mechanism is represented by a few bolts and traces of brickwork, not very overgrown. The leat is well preserved and can be traced about a quarter of a mile to the upper pond. Although now in filled, the pond shape can be made out. It was retained by an earth bank and would have provided about a 30 foot head. The lower pool has also been drained, but the former dam remains as an embankment carrying a road. Both outflows are in good condition. The 1806 account describes a 20 feet diameter water wheel at the lower works, 10 feet wide, which worked various rolls and sheers. A particularly interesting feature is a branched stone culvert that must have emptied into the lower pool. The main part of the tunnel heads under the pool, perhaps acting as an overflow within that pool from the forge buildings and may have been a tailrace from the upper mill" (Poyner.2008).

He records in *Transactions 1999*, the mouth of the tunnel lies beside what was the lower pond under a tree root, there is a stone retaining wall on the east side which is about 6 feet long. The tunnel is in good condition and stretches for about 50 feet approximately, due north until it is blocked by a fall. There is also a branch tunnel but is also blocked, both tunnels appear to be in good condition and although mysterious, he suggests that they may have been used

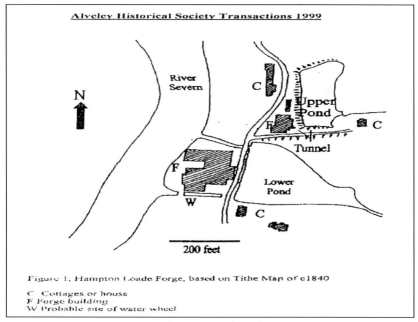

Figure 31 Hampton Loade Forge, taken from *Transactions 1999*.

for water conservation. He says" The smaller tunnel seems to be heading in the direction of the forge itself [...] It is possible that water from the upper pond was sent to the forge for some purpose and then redirected to the lower pool [...] It seems likely that it was the outlet from the lower pond that drove the water wheel that is known to have existed at the site. It would have been important to ensure that the lower pond always had enough water to drive the We now know that there was a furnace on the site of the iron works much earlier than was previously considered, Poyner's work details dates of the furnace which had been in existence for several years by the time of the 1647 document mentioned, it seems likely that the furnace must have been built about 1641.

He also notes that this would make Hampton a contemporary of a number of other Shropshire furnaces. The next mention of Hampton comes in 1653, when Thomas Whitmore paid £13-2-6 for 1 ton 6cwt 1qr of "cast necessaries from Hampton Loade" (appendix 1). Whitmore was probably a member of the local Whitmore family originating from Apley, north of Bridgnorth.

The final direct reference to Hampton Loade furnace comes in 1662, with the survival of a receipt for £1 for the casting of pots and other objects by John

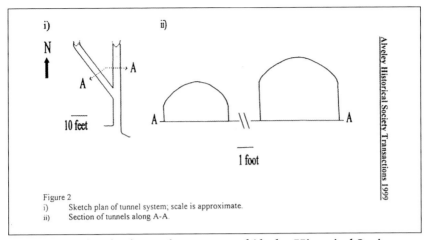

Figure 2
i)   Sketch plan of tunnel system; scale is approximate.
ii)   Section of tunnels along A-A.

Figure 32 **Sketch of tunnels, courtesy of Alveley Historical Society.**

Legas at Hampton Loade, Grange and Coven furnaces (the latter two being in Staffordshire). Legas first appears in the locality in 1648 when he baptised his son Richard at Chelmarsh: his work meant that he often had to travel away from Highley. In fact it seems unlikely that Hampton Loade furnace was still working in 1668. The works were not transferred to Philip Foley and the detailed accounts that survive from that and subsequent years do not mention a furnace at Hampton Loade. If the furnace had been granted to Foley on a standard 21 year lease, this would have expired in 1662, making this the most likely date for its closure (Poyner.2009).

Poyner concludes that "I believe much can still be discovered about the earlier phases of the iron industry at Hampton Loade, both from research in the archives and in a special survey on the ground" (2000). He also concludes in his article on Hampton Loade's Top Mill paper:

> "Hampton Loade Top Mill represents an unexpected survival of an intact building from the forge. It may well have been part of the original forge of c1783. Further study of the building and its surrounding areas might provide more clues as to the history of the site and also of wrought iron production when it was subject to a period of intense technical experimentation. Thus it may be of more than mere local significance" (Poyner.2009).

We still have no proof as to who built the bridge or when, however, given the ever growing information from locals, Poyner and Hayman, we know that pieces of the jigsaw are still being discovered and we should not presume that we know all there is to know, that vital piece is there somewhere waiting to be found.

Figure 33 **Vestiges of the old iron works.**

Figure 34 **Top Mill Hampton Loade during restoration, showing where the wheel was formerly positioned.**

Figure 35 **Top Mill before renovation.**

Figure 36 **Hampton Loade below Top Mill.**

Newspaper article 20th March 1854

Hamptons Loade Mill

In the parish of Chelmarsh

Nock and Wilson

Will sell by Auction on

Monday 20th March 1854

Household Furniture

Rick of hay to go off; Milking cow; Four store pigs; Poultry

130 gallons of cider; Brewing and dairy vessels & co

The property of Mr Page who is leaving Hampton Loade

The sale is to commence at 12.00 o'clock punctually.

Figure 37 **For sale notice of a mill in Hampton Loade 1854.**

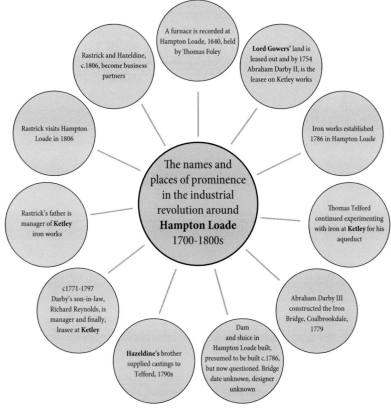

Figure 38 **The prominent names of the industrial revolution sit comfortably beside Hampton Loade.**

The constant force of change in Hampton Loade

The cottages, Top Mill, the Old Forge House and the Mission Hall in the hamlet mentioned in the personal account by Les Link, are all now private dwellings. The site close to the river has been renamed as the Old Smithy and owners of the property over the years have tended and restored the walls which once housed the works, it currently serves as a garden although it is soon to become a site for more caravan homes. These remnants of the past retain the charm and atmosphere of the past without the noise which would once have reverberated around the valley and the heat which could be felt all year round. The massive reservoir stretching into the wooded valley which once powered the water wheels is long gone, no longer needed to blow forced air through huge bellows into the furnaces and to power the hammers to knock off the slag from the ingots. The only vestige of the reservoir is now the pond which is home to the ducks and wildlife behind The River and Rail public House.

Joyce Cooper's mother Nancy Gwilt, occupied 16 Hampton Loade, Joyce's father was born in the same house. Courtesy of Alveley Historical Society.

The Severn Valley Railway Station at Hampton Loade: The Country Station

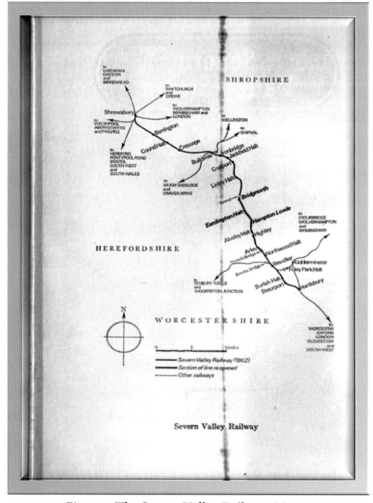

Figure 39 **The Severn Valley Railway, Map.**

The Story of the Severn Valley Railway begins when Parliament agreed that the original Severn Valley Railway SVR) could be built, however it was to be another nine years before the dream became a reality. Once it was finished it proved to be a vital link between Worcester and Shrewsbury, town and country and commerce with agriculture. Along the nearly forty mile line there were thirteen stations, the village of Hampton Loade being one of them.

The Severn valley Railway line, from Bridgnorth to Kidderminster, was opened in 1862 and closed in 1963 at around the time of Dr Beechings cuts, although it had been planned for closure before the report was produced. Hampton Loade was one of the first to be restored by volunteers in 1970. The tranquil stretch of track from Hampton Loade to Arley hosting the station which justifiably earns its name as the 'Country Station'. Should you choose to take this sedate journey on the steam train where the closed carriages will gently rock you back to 1945, the upholstery remains unadorned with graffiti and the windows blow the outside breeze in for comfort without the aid of air con-

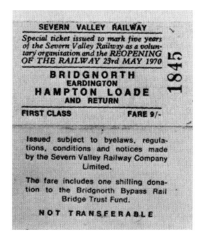

ditioning. It is a pleasant journey where the uniformed guard will politely help you on your way, usually an enthusiastic volunteer, proud of his place on a historic route which was recreated for the visitor in 1970. On a quiet day if you are fortunate enough for the sun to shine through the widows and dress for one of the forties themed events, the transformation back to a more gentle age will be complete.

The station at Hampton Loade is a nostalgic addition to the trip and if you should alight here, you will find a beautifully kept, flower filled step in to an era largely lost to us now. Painted picket fences and a model railway enthral the visitor old and young alike, a tactile experience, nostalgia to be seen, smelled and enjoyed, this is genuine history to fill all your senses and not just your fingertips, the interactive game has never visited here. An ice cream from the kiosk or refreshments in the tea room complete the experience. For me it is *Brief Encounter* of another kind and is whole heartedly forgiven for opening in 1863, when it suffered more than a little opposition at the time for scarring the country side and killing off all the river traffic and working barges. It's now a delightful journey, no longer scarring but gently soothing its passengers on a day out, long may it continue.

Following closure by British Rail in 1963, all signalling equipment was removed from Hampton Loade, and the signal box was, more or less, completely demolished. The station has been used as the filming location for *The Englishmen Who Went up a Hill but came down a Mountain*, starring Hugh Grant and *Mad Dogs*, a 1970's serial.

Station masters remembered

William Sherwood 1895.

Alfred Stanley 1917.

Joseph Thomas Hill 1922.

Henry Powell 1879.

Mr S Docherty, assisted by Mr R Dodd, both appointed in 1999. Fred Hughes is the chief Booking Clerk.

Mr C. Walton is the station master and Mr. Thomas is the assistant station master, 2009.

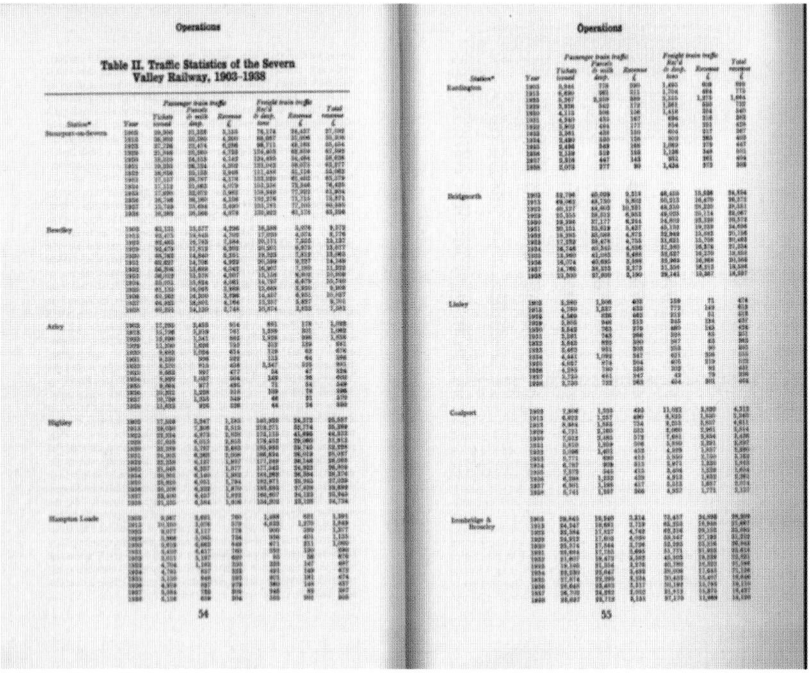

Operations

Table II. Traffic Statistics of the Severn Valley Railway, 1903-1938

54

Operations

55

Figure 40 **Timetable for The Severn Valley Railway.**

The Severn Valley Railway provided four passenger trains each way daily between Shrewsbury and Bridgnorth. On 18 July 1872, the SVR was absorbed into the Great Western Railway which in 1878 opened a link between Kidderminster and Bewdley, which created another vital link, this time between the West Midlands and the Severn Valley.

By the 1930s, despite increasing competition from the motor car, five trains were running daily from Hartlebury or Kidderminster to Shrewsbury.

Figure 41 **The train pulls in at Hampton Loade.**

Fortunately The Severn Valley Railway Society was formed on 6 July 1965, when a group of enthusiasts met at Kidderminster to assess the possibility of keeping the line open. The society intended to run passenger trains from Bridgnorth to Hampton Loade, just over 4 miles. A price of £25,000 was agreed with British Rail to cover all freehold land, buildings and track, which, thanks to fund-raising efforts, was collected in 3 years. On Saturday 23 May 1970, the first public passenger train left Bridgnorth for Hampton Loade and back with an hourly service following.

A succession of campaigns sponsored by various rail enthusiasts enabled the final goal of reaching Kidderminster: the line now carries in excess of 240,000 passengers annually. Work to construct Kidderminster Town station buildings began later in 1984 thanks to a grant of £60,000 from the English Tourist Board. It was completed in stages and was officially opened to the public on 4 July 1986.

Figure 42 **Hampton Loade Station.**

A sad undated event at Hampton Loade station

An infant's body was found wrapped in brown paper on the train at Hampton Loade. The body was found in the third class compartments on the luggage racks after complaints of a peculiar odour was said to be permeating the carriages. The investigating officer said that no more investigations were necessary. The infant's body was taken to Shrewsbury mortuary.

The Unicorn Inn

The Unicorn Inn stands on the same side as The Hampton Loade station; it has stood the test of time over many years and has a few tales to tell, some of which are included here. It now enjoys a loyal following from fishermen, campers, walkers and locals.

A spot of bother at Hampton Loade, Shropshire in 1856, Published by kind permission of Rhys Whatmore

If your ancestor was an agricultural laborer you would not expect him to be mentioned in the local newspaper unless he had been involved in criminal activities, so when a friend at Shropshire Archives told me that she had found a James Whatmore of Hampton in Chelmarsh parish, Shropshire, mentioned in the issue of the 'Shrewsbury Chronicle' for 25 July 1856, I wondered what on earth he had been up to. This James Whatmore was born at Bewdley in 1795 and died at Hampton in Chelmarsh parish in 1877 and was my great great great grandfather.

Figure 43
The Unicorn Inn.

The news item turned out to be a report of a court action brought by Mr Martin (plaintiff) against Mr James Randall (defendant) for the sum of £20 2s 9d of which £2 6s 8d had already been paid into the court.

Mr Martin kept an Inn and a malt house at Hampton Loade. Mr Randall was a wool stapler at Kidderminster.

The Unicorn Inn at Hampton Loade was run by John Martin in the 1850s

Mr Randall had taken on a farm at Hampton Loade for three years, from Mr Whitmore's agent. [This would be Mr Whitmore, the local magnate who lived at nearby Dudmaston Hall. There is no connection between this Mr Whitmore and the Whatmore family]. It had been Mr Randall's intention that his son John William Randall should look after the farm.

It was claimed that it had been agreed that Mr Martin should supply malt and other necessities for the farm which he had done to the value of £10 11s 9d. It was further claimed that on Mr. Randall's behalf, Mr Martin had hired a threshing machine for three separate seasons at a total cost of £8. Mr Martin was also claiming £1- 13s - 1½d for the use of the ferry boat for Mr. Randall, his servants and his cattle. He had further supplied beer to the value of £1- 3s to Mr Randall's servants and had paid 15s 4½d as tax for a dog owned by Mr Randall.

There was some argument in court about who had ordered the malt and authorized the other expenditure and about who was responsible for the debt. To quote directly from the news report:

'James Whatmore, a laborer, said that he had been engaged by the defendant to work on the farm at Hampton Loade and to look after the sheep. The son was on the farm but defendant said that he would not look after them. Defendant used to pay the wages and he did so for some months. After then, the son sometimes paid. Witness worked on the farm about 12 months, when he left. After being away a year he went again and the wages were paid sometimes by Miss Randall and sometimes by defendant. In December 1854 the stock and furniture on the farm were sold. In answer to Mr Huddleston [Counsel for the defendant] witness said the sheep were marked J W R by order of the son who had the mark made. Could not say how the carts and wagons were marked'

Mr James Randall, defendant, explained to the court that he had taken the farm from Mr Whitmore's agent but had had nothing to do with the running of the farm until November 1853 when his son had run away. Mr James Randall denied ever asking Mr Martin to supply malt. He said that Mr Martin had never told him that his son owned him money. Mr James Randall claimed that the debts were his son's.

To cut short a long newspaper account, the jury after a brief consultation, returned a verdict for the plaintiff, deducting the 15s 4½d for the dog tax.

In reading this account one is unsure who displayed the greatest naivety – Mr Martin for supplying goods and incurring expenditure without securities, or Mr Randall Senior for trusting an apparently untrustworthy son.

The Unicorn Inn is located near the river Severn on the west bank and still exists today. The 1851 census shows the occupants as John Martin Innkeeper, aged 35 born Wrockwardine, his wife Mary Ann aged 30 born Glazeley, 4 children, 2 servants and 2 travelers. 1851 James Whatmore was living close by, also on the west bank. It is possible, however, from the references to the use of the ferry that the farm referred to in the court case was on the east bank of the river. Although the name Hampton Loade is given for the location of the farm and the Inn, technically Hampton Loade is on the east bank and the hamlet on the west bank is called Hampton (previously 'Hempton'). The confusion was not helped by the decision to name the station built in the nineteenth century on the Severn Valley railway line, 'Hampton Loade Station', even though it is located on the west bank.

The 'Hampton Loade' ferry still exists, the last working ferry in Shropshire on the river Severn. It is well worth a visit as is a trip on the steam operated Severn Valley Railway which runs from Bridgnorth to Kidderminster".

The Shropshire News 1911

"Henry Hayward was caught stealing fowl on March 18th 1911. On the following day his brother William Henry Hayward was caught stealing from the Unicorn Public house and was fined for assaulting Mr. John Jones from the Unicorn Public house with an iron[ing]"?

Mr. John Jones told the court The Hayward's were notorious in the area for stealing, poaching and adultery. It was not just the men in the family either , cousin Sarah stayed just six months in the village and managed to take home the prospect of a new mouth to feed. Sadly her father didn't want the child either and so she returned only to be told there was 'no room at the Inn'. Court records show a row broke out between the brothers, at The Unicorn Inn but it is Sarah that ends up punished for causing the disturbance. Records show that ever resourceful and quick witted Sarah survives the ordeal and moves on, she is later listed with no child working alone at a public house, whilst the newspapers still mention of the brothers as in the vicinity.

A walk around Hampton Loade

The ferry .

Figure 44 **Woodcock Lodge Hampton Loade courtesy of Hilary Fewtrell.**

Bibliography

Books

Alveley Historical Association, *Images of Alveley*.1999. Alan J. Nicholls (Honiton).

Cossons, Neil. Trinder Barrie. *The Iron Bridge, Symbol of the Industrial Revolution*. Severn Valley Railway. *From The Window*. 2008.

Nicholls, Alan, James. *The History of Alveley*. A. Nicholls 1994.

Raistrick, Arthur. *Dynasty of Ironfounders*. David & Charles 1970.

Rose, Alan. *Shropshire Inn signs*. Tempus. 2006.

Trinder, Barrie. *The Industrial Revolution in Shropshire*. Chichester Phillimore. 2000.

Whittle, Rob. *Hampton Loade 1790s to 2003*.

Journals

Shropshire Archives. *Leases of Hampton Loade ironworks*. 5586/5/4/8. *The Journal of the Wilkinson Society. No. 17: 1995 2004-8*. 2009.

Mutton, Norman. *'The Foster Family: a study of a Midland industrial dynasty 1786 1899'* (thesis 1973: Dudley Archives and Local History Centre).

English Heritage Advice Report. 18 Jan 2010. *Cast Iron Bridge, Alveley*. Parish Alveley Case UID: 161615 District Bridgnorth County Shropshire. 11-May-2006.

Alveley Historical Society.1999. *Transactions of the Shropshire Archaeological and History Society, pp 235-243*.

Alveley Historical Society.1995. *Transactions of the Shropshire Archaeological and History Society*.

Electronic sources

The Llangollen Canal http://www.canaljunction.com/ canal/llangollen.htm accessed 14.01.2010.

'Ketley: Economic history', A History of the County of Shropshire: Volume 11: Telford 1985), pp. 269-273. URL: http://www.british-history.ac.uk/ report.aspx?compid= 18161 Date accessed: 14 January 2010.

Poyner, David. *The Mills of Alveley and Romsley. Shropshire article*. http://www. oldcopper.org.uk/ Broseley/17.htm#_Toc50196155. Date accessed: 11.November. 2009.

Poyner, David. *Hampton Loade Furnace*. www.shropshirehistory.org.uk/html /resource: 2009. *1105152910*. Date accessed: 7 April 2010.

Ricardo, David. *The Works and Correspondence of David Ricardo, ed. Piero Sraffa with the Collaboration of M.H. Dobb (Indianapolis: Liberty Fund, 2005). Vol. 5 Speeches and Evidence 1815-1823*. Chapter: Mr. Whitmore's motion respecting the Corn Laws. 26 February 1823. Accessed from http://oll.libertyfund.org/title/ 206/38837 Date accessed: 12 January 2009.

Hayman, Richard. *The Shropshire wrought-iron industry c1600-1900: a study of technological change*. Ph.D. thesis, University of Birmingham. (2004). http://etheses.bham.ac.uk/248/1/ Hayman04PhD_A1a.pdf 26th March 2010.

Index